The Secret of
Shay Cho Bay

by Mereline Griffith

Mereline G. ♡

.... follow the dragonfly ......

Copyright © 2014 by Mereline Griffith
First Edition — May 2014

Illustrations by Susan Lynes
Reviewed by Brenda Kissel
Back Cover Photograph by Mereline Griffith

ISBN
978-1-4602-3873-8 (Paperback)
978-1-4602-3874-5 (eBook)

All rights reserved.

No part of this publication may be reproduced in any form, or by any means, electronic or mechanical, including photocopying, recording, or any information browsing, storage, or retrieval system, without permission in writing from the publisher.

Produced by:

FriesenPress

Suite 300 – 852 Fort Street
Victoria, BC, Canada V8W 1H8

www.friesenpress.com

Distributed to the trade by The Ingram Book Company

Many thanks to Susan for the charming illustrations, to Brenda for reviewing and advice on writing for children, to friends, family and my "Underground Writing Cohorts" Suzanne, Shannon, Kelly, Sara and Marilynne, who encouraged me to carry this story through to publishing. Merci Jeannette, for inspiring me to write.

An early morning walk on the beach is the best way to start the day. This is the quiet time. It's the time before all the people noises begin. It's the best time to connect with nature.

Morning at the lake is a good time to find pretty rocks. It's a good time to find interesting driftwood, or other bric-a-brac. These things may have washed up on the beach overnight.

On this special morning, I step out the door. A warm, friendly sun greets me. It feels good on my face. It makes me smile.

Whenever I walk on the beach, I get puzzled. I see strange little tracks in the sand. Who made them? Was it a small creature, dragging something behind it?

It's a real mystery. The tiny tracks go up the shore to the grass. Then they come back down. The water washes them away like a well-kept secret.

Joyful little wavelets ripple into shore. Then they ripple out again…always moving. They leave pretty patterns in the wet sand.

I watch the wavelets. I wonder…do they know the secret? I decide they do know. They are the ones who wiped the tracks away.

A big owl settles down on a high branch to sleep. He fluffs his feathers. He looks down and winks once. He knows the secret. But then owls always know stuff. That's why they are called "wise owls."

Out on the water, I spot a pontoon boat. I see my neighbors on it. We wave to each other as the big boat cruises by. My neighbors' grandson is with them. He's wearing his bright-red life jacket. I can tell he is enjoying his early morning ride on the lake. He's wearing the biggest smile.

On the dock, I stop to visit a school of mini-fish. The fish like to hang out there at this time of day. Round and round they swim. They gulp their breakfast on the go. They are keeping an eye out for bigger fish. The big fish might want them for breakfast. When I see a school of fish; I always wonder; *Which one is the teacher?* This morning I wonder; *Do these fish know the secret?* Of course they do.

Taking my shoes off, I walk on. I enjoy the special sounds of the lakeshore. On the calmest day, a gentle breeze still blows through the grass. This morning it seems to be saying — *Seeeecret…*

The Lakeshore Society of Seagulls is up early as usual. The seagulls noisily argue over their breakfast. Some careless person has left french-fries on the beach. Seagulls are very vocal. Today, their gossip is mixed with high-pitched, seagull laughter…Even the silly seagulls know the secret. But I'm still wondering.

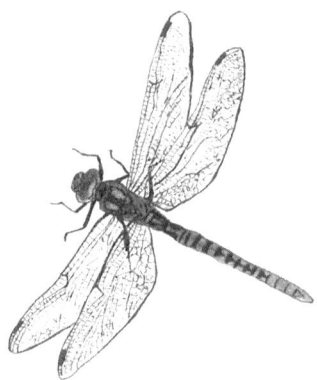

Now I feel sad. The wavelets know the secret. The wise owl knows the secret. The fish and the silly seagulls are in on the secret. Even the wind knows and I don't…

The call of a loon turns my attention to the lake. A mother loon swims along the shore. Her baby chick is riding on her back. Awwwww…it's so cute, I forget to be sad.

There are so many wonderful things to see and hear at the lakeshore. It doesn't really matter if I know the secret. I walk back along the beach. The smile returns to my face. I just feel happy again.

Then — I look up ahead. I see what I have been looking for all morning. Slowly and surely, something makes its way along the beach. It leaves tiny tracks in the sand.

Can you guess what it is?

IT IS A TURTLE!

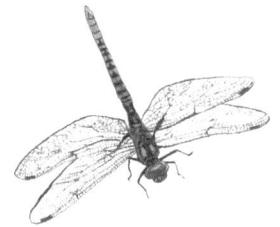

I am so excited!

Out on the lake, the fish jump. The loon laughs. The seagulls cheer, in their high-pitched voices. The big, wise owl looks down. He stretches and winks twice. The wavelets wave, the wind whistles, and I have learned the secret.

Now you know the secret too.

The True Story

A turtle really did live on the beach at Moose Lake's Shay Cho Bay. We know that she was a female, because she was seen laying her eggs on the beach.

Where she came from is a mystery because Moose Lake is not a natural habitat for turtles of any kind.

This story of the Turtle of Shay Cho Bay is a tiny bit of local history, and may help to share and preserve the inspiring story of a small creature, which was somehow misplaced and forced to live in a new and different environment, but survived anyway.

Viv Blackburn photo

The Turtle has not been seen for several years. I believe she has just moved on after her beach home became too busy. I hope that somewhere; she has found a new (secret) home along the shores of beautiful Moose Lake. There, she may be living in harmony with nature; joyfully swimming with the mini-fish, laughing with the silly seagulls, and slowly, quietly, walking along the beach…leaving strange little tracks in the sand.

About the Author

Ashley Hempel Photography

Mereline Griffith's previous publications include two poetry collections and a family memoir. *The Secret of Shay Cho Bay* is her first children's story. Mereline resides near Bonnyville, Alberta.

About the Illustrator

Susan Lynes, who lives in the Bonnyville area in northeast Alberta, has been drawing and painting for many years. She was delighted when Mereline asked her to create the drawings for "The Secret of Shay Cho Bay." This is her first time illustrating a book.